Con

Minute Motivators for Graduates

Stan Toler

HONOR HB BOOKS

Inspiration and Motivation for the Seasons of Life

COOK COMMUNICATIONS MINISTRIES
Colorado Springs, Colorado • Paris, Ontario
KINGSWAY COMMUNICATIONS LTD
Eastbourne, England

Honor Books® is an imprint of
Cook Communications Ministries, Colorado Springs, CO 80918
Cook Communications, Paris, Ontario
Kingsway Communications, Eastbourne, England

MINUTE MOTIVATORS FOR MEN
© 2004 by STAN TOLER

First printing, 2004
Printed in the United States of America
3 4 5 6 7 Printing/Year 09 08 07 06 05

Developed by Bordon Books
6532 E. 71st Street, Suite 105
Tulsa, OK 74133

ISBN: 1-56292-231-0

Introduction

That step off the platform of your graduation ceremony is the longest—and most important—step of your life. Your family and friends may loudly cheer when you receive your diploma; but later on—after you've turned in your rented graduation robe—you may stand alone in a deafening silence. What now? You'll need to find some fast answers to some pretty heavy questions. In the next weeks, months, and years, you'll face demands that make your classroom assignments look simple by comparison.

Minute Motivators for Graduates is not a book with *all* of the answers. It's a book with *some* of the answers. There are no cookie-cutter principles here, no template for life. Just practical, powerful, and helpful hints for turning the first days of the rest of your life into something powerful and productive.

Congratulations on the start of a fantastic journey!

Stan Toler

Focus on the future.

"Vision for your future is the road map of what God wants to accomplish in and through you."

—Jim Williams

VISION

Where do you want to be in five years? In ten years? In twenty?

Many high school or college students don't think much beyond the next weekend. They're focused on what's in front of them today, right now.

You don't have that luxury. You're a graduate now. That means, for the most part, your life is in your own hands. The direction you take at this intersection could be a road to success or a dead end.

What are you dreaming? God often puts dreams in our hearts for what He has planned for us.

Will you be happily married? Will you have a successful career? Will you be a parent? An artist? A doctor? A builder? Let the vision take shape in your mind. Determine now what your future could be.

Of course, life doesn't always follow a script. It's improvisation. But plan anyway. Every successful venture usually begins with a plan—in business, in sports, or in the arts. Vision is the deciding factor and the winning factor.

You have a great future. Can you see it?

Prepare for the future.

"Good plans shape good decisions."

—Lester R. Bittel

PLANNING

I love the game of golf, but it's challenging. Most of the time I have trouble getting the ball to go in the right direction. No matter how carefully I aim, the ball often lands somewhere else.

The game of life is different. In life, you usually hit what you're aiming for.

That means you can land wherever you choose. If you want an education, you can aim for it and get one. It may not be easy, but you can do it.

If you want a career, you can have one, but you must plan for it. Success doesn't grow on trees; you have to aim for it. Make a plan, and then make it happen.

Of course, there's a downside. Since you hit whatever you aim for, you must aim carefully. If you aim at nothing, you will hit nothing. Those who waste money, squander opportunities, and ruin relationships are planning a difficult and painful life; and they are never disappointed.

Watch where you're going!

Learn from your mistakes.

"The difference between
average people and
achieving people is their
perspective of failure."

—John Maxwell

FAILURE

Here's a prediction that is guaranteed to come true: you will fail. Everyone fails. It's inevitable. It's part of being human. The worst response to failure is to become discouraged or even worse, to quit. But failure isn't fatal. In fact, it can be a valuable experience when you learn from it.

Some of your failures will be small. You'll fail to turn in a report on time and be scolded by your boss. That experience will teach you to manage your time, and you'll be better for it.

Other failures may be more painful. You may break a promise to someone you care about and lose an important relationship. That situation will hurt, but you'll discover the value of faithfulness and gain a life lesson.

Each failure is an opportunity to grow. Don't plan to fail, but plan to learn from your mistakes. You have one degree under your belt, but there's another one coming, a graduate course in the school of hard knocks.

There are no scholarships offered for this degree!

Don't burn your bridges.

"There is nothing on this earth more to be prized than true friendship."

—Saint Thomas Aquinas

RELATIONSHIPS

What's the most valuable commodity in the world? Gold? Oil? Precious stones? Cash? No!

All of the above have value, but none is as important as the greatest treasure on earth—relationships.

The people in your life are the most precious asset you have. Your parents, relatives, coworkers, fellow students, and friends—these are your gold mine.

Don't squander them.

It will be tempting to quit a job where the supervisor is mean and demanding. Leave if you must, but leave on good terms. You may need the goodwill of the company and the cranky boss in the future.

Friends may break promises or behave selfishly. Remember that no one is perfect. You have failed others, too. Make every effort to repair a damaged friendship.

At the end of your life, you will not be concerned with the things you have achieved, or the things you have owned. What will matter is the people in your life who have helped you, befriended you, and brought you joy.

Keep the bridge of friendship in good repair.

Attend church faithfully.

"Write your plans in pencil,
but give God the eraser."

—Anonymous

SPIRITUALITY

Look at yourself in the mirror. What do you see? Now look deeper. Look inside your eyes. What's in there?

You're more than you appear to be on the outside. Your physical body is not the real you. The real person is the one inside, the spirit that inhabits your body.

You are a spiritual being; that's the way God made you. And that means that you have spiritual, not just physical, needs.

To take care of your body, you eat the right foods, rest, and get plenty of exercise. But how do you take care of your spiritual health?

One of the best ways is to gather with other people who believe in God and worship Him together. In other words, go to church.

Church is the only place on earth that is devoted exclusively to your spiritual health. It is the best resource available to you for worship, spiritual growth, and fellowship with other believers.

If you pencil church into your schedule, you won't need your eraser as much.

Manage
your minutes.

"Always remember
that the future comes
one day at a time."

—Dean Acheson

TIME

Every day, you get paid 1,440 minutes. That's more than 10,000 minutes a week. You're mega wealthy!

So tell me, what are you going to spend your precious time on today? Sleeping? That's about 480 minutes. Work? That's another 480 or so. What about the rest?

Imagine minutes were dollars. Would you watch television for four hours today if it cost you $240? Would you play video games for two hours if you had to rent the machine for $120?

Your minutes are more valuable than money. And your success depends largely on how you manage your time. Minutes are the building blocks of your life. You use them to construct whatever you wish. But they can also be wasted. Wasted money can always be regained. Wasted minutes are gone forever.

Budget your time just as you budget your money. Spend your time in the areas of highest priority. Time with God, time with your family, time with your friends, and time spent helping others should be at the top of your list. Sometimes your spent time will include watching television, chatting with friends, or just hanging out. Plan your days—even your days off—so that you accomplish what is most important. You don't want to rush the time you have with those you love.

Got a minute? You're a millionaire!

Be patient in decision making.

"Nobody ever did, or ever will,
escape the consequences
of his choices."

—Alfred A. Montapert

CHOICES

What's the first thing you will do after graduation? Buy a car? Travel? Get married?

Hold the phone! Take your time with those choices. Buying a new car will tie up a large part of your income for several years. Are you sure you want to do that?

Getting married is a great idea, if you're prepared. Have you chosen the right life partner? Do you have a job lined up? How will this decision affect your future education?

Be patient when you make decisions, especially those that have long-term consequences. The things you hope to do are probably good, and no doubt you will do them. The real question is when to get started. Ask God if He has any plans that you haven't thought of for your life. Often He has plans so awesome you cannot imagine them.

Make a plan. Factor in the financial, social, physical, and spiritual elements. Then work your plan. Go ahead and hit the "Enter" button on the keyboard of your life. But keep an eye on the monitor. Choose your keystrokes carefully. You'll achieve all that you hope to. But it may take longer than you first thought.

Choose right, and you'll be all right.

Respect
God's creation.

"It's not good enough that
we do our best; sometimes we
have to do what is required."

—Winston Churchill

CREATION

There is a God, and He created the world.

Such a statement may seem obvious to some, yet, incredibly, many people lose sight of that rather simple fact. Surrounded by manmade structures and human chatter, it's easy to forget that there is a natural, bountiful created world and an even more bountiful Creator who stands behind it.

Because we live in a world of God's making, we must respect both Him and the gift He has given us.

Show your respect for the Creator by acknowledging that your own body is a gift. Treat it with care. Don't abuse it with alcohol, tobacco, or harmful drugs. Keep fit by maintaining a proper diet and getting plenty of rest and exercise.

Show your respect for the Creator by treating the world He has given us with care. Be a careful consumer, never wasting the precious resources that enhance our lives. Reduce the amount of refuse you produce, and reuse or recycle as many things as you can.

Most of all, show your respect for the Creator by honoring His Word. He has given us ten unalterable commandments by which to live. Obey God by obeying these commandments.

God has given us all we need to live healthy and productive lives. Do it!

Don't be afraid to ask questions.

"A moment's insight
is sometimes worth
a life's experience."

—Oliver Wendall Holmes

INSIGHT

Someone once said, "There's no such thing as a stupid question." It's true!

Most educational systems reward knowledge. The people who don't know the answers receive lower grades. That makes some of us afraid to ask questions for fear of revealing our ignorance. After all, nobody wants to look stupid.

But life in the real world is different than in school. Out here, performance is rewarded. The person who can get the job done moves ahead. And to do that, you need to get the information necessary to be effective.

Nobody is born with all the answers. That's obvious from some of the people you've met along the way! Pretending to know it all doesn't add to performance—only to pride.

Every achievement in life, whether in science, arts, industry, or sports, began with an inquiring mind. Someone wasn't afraid to get a little more information on the subject.

Ignorance is scarier than a question.

Cultivate the habit of listening.

"No man ever listened himself out of a job."

—Calvin Coolidge

LISTENING

It's easy to spot a know-it-all. That's the one person in any group who is always talking.

A *real* know-it-all, someone who really does have wisdom, is easy to spot too. That's the person who usually spends more time listening than talking.

It's amazing what you can find out when you take the time to listen.

"I don't have to diagnose my patients," one doctor said. "They diagnose themselves. All I have to do is listen carefully when they tell me about themselves." It's the same in all areas of life. Listeners are learners. And learners are winners.

Listen to your friends; you'll find out about their dreams. Listen to your coworkers; you'll learn to do your own job better. Listen to your parents; you can learn from their mistakes. Listen to your boyfriend or girlfriend; you'll discover their character. And listen to God; He's always communicating His love and attention to His children.

Everything you need to know, someone will tell you. But you must be willing to listen.

"Listen up" is more than a word of advice; it's a life direction.

Never be paralyzed by fear.

"A true friend knows your weaknesses but shows your strengths; feels your fears but fortifies your faith."

—William Arthur Ward

FEARS

Only one thing stands between you and your dreams, fear. Before you can conquer the world, you must conquer yourself; overcoming the fear that keeps you from stepping out, taking risks, and moving toward your goals.

Fear of failure keeps us from starting a new project.

Fear of losing keeps us from winning.

Fear of dying keeps us from really living.

There's a big, wonderful world out there. It is a world of opportunity, but also a world of risk. A world of possibility, but also a world of obstacles. A world that is yours for the taking. But to conquer it, you must be willing to face your worst enemy, the paralysis of fear. God would love to give you the strength and courage to face your next problem, if you would just ask Him for help. "Help" is often the easiest prayer to say.

You might not win an Olympic gold medal today. But you can learn how to pace yourself for the long run. It's the little steps you take today that will give you courage for the big leap tomorrow.

T-R-Y is a three-letter word, but it trumps the four-letter word F-E-A-R.

Finish what you start.

"Kites rise highest against
the wind, not with it."

—Winston Churchill

DETERMINATION

In trying to perfect the revolutionary piece of technology, the light bulb, inventor Thomas Edison conducted more than a thousand experiments. Nearly all of them failed. Somewhere along the line, a reporter asked Edison what he had learned from one thousand failed experiments. He said, "I've learned one thousand ways not to invent the light bulb."

We live in a brighter world because Edison conducted experiment number 1,001! It's that same kind of determination that will keep you out of the dark. Never give up. Your life is worth too much to leave it half finished. God will never give up on you. Don't give up on Him.

If you begin a higher education degree, finish it. You'll be glad you did. If you start a job, see it through to the end. You'll always regret what you leave undone. If you begin working on a personal discipline, stick to it. With a little bit of personal effort, you can do it. Finish what you start.

Determination may start with a "D," but it will give you an "A" on your finals.

Practice giving living.

"That's what I consider true
generosity! You give your all,
and yet you always feel
as if it cost you nothing."

—Simone de Beauvoir

GENEROSITY

You've heard the saying, "What goes around, comes around." It's true. You get what you give in this life. That goes double for the generous person.

When you are generous, others notice and return the favor. The same concept applies when you are stingy. Lend a hand, and someone will return the favor when you're in need. Pitch in on a tough project, and someone will help you when you're under a deadline. Give twenty dollars to a friend in need, and you'll make a friend for life. But your choice to give shouldn't be dictated by the desire for friends or help in the future—although that is an added perk. Your generosity will ultimately result in a much bigger prize—joy. There is a natural delight in helping others that will spread to all areas of your life.

Generosity isn't a natural thing. It takes work. Like running, it is a life habit. And you cultivate it the way you cultivate any other life skill, by practice.

Jesus said, "Give and it will be given to you," and He was right. Make giving the habit of your life, and you'll receive far more in return. Start small, if you have to, but start.

If all you have to give someone is a break, then start with that, and work your way up to a twenty!

Always pray for God's will.

"Trust in the Lord with all your heart and lean not on your own understanding; in all your ways acknowledge him and he will make your paths straight."

—Proverbs 3:5-6

GUIDANCE

You don't have to make tough decisions all by yourself. Someone who loves you more than you'll ever know will teach you everything you'll ever need to know.

Some are fortunate to have one or more parents who are a source of guidance and inspiration. But there is an even higher source of wisdom than an earthly parent. There is a heavenly father, God.

You have an open invitation to approach the Keeper of the universe with your earthly problems. And He'll never blow you off!

It's as simple as holding a conversation:

"Heavenly Father, I'm confused. I don't know which way to turn. . . ."

"Lord, I've failed, but I'm not sure how to make it right. . . ."

"God, I want to do what's right, but I'm not sure what that is. . . ."

God's Word, the Bible, tells us that if anyone lacks wisdom, he should ask God for it (James 1:5). He not only knows everything, He also loves us tremendously and wants to help us with our problems.

You don't have to go it alone. He's already been where you're thinking about going.

Put God first.

"Decide what you want;
decide what you are willing
to exchange for it. Establish
your priorities and go to work."

—H. L. Hunt

PRIORITIES

What's the most important thing in your life? Earning a good income? Finishing graduate school? Getting married?

All of those choices are good things, but they are not the most important things in life.

The secret to a successful life is to put things in order, or to have right priorities. And the first priority is God. There's a shelf in your heart reserved for Him. When He's there, everything else is in its proper place.

Put God first in your spiritual life. He created you, and He wants you to find a life of happiness and contentment. Get to know Him by praying and reading His Word, the Bible.

Put God first in your social life. Worship with your friends, your family, or your boyfriend or girlfriend. Go to church every week.

Put God first in your financial life. Honor Him by giving a tithe, ten percent of your income for His work. And give more to others in need, as you meet them.

Put God first in your professional life. Conduct your work with integrity and honesty.

If God's on first, all the other bases will be covered.

Stay in touch with old friends.

"A true friend never gets
in your way unless you
happen to be going down."

—Arnold H. Glasow

FRIENDSHIPS

Most likely your lifelong friends will be those who are your friends right now. They're the ones who know you best, love you most, and will be loyal to you throughout your life. Hold on to those friendships.

Right now, your friends are mostly for fun. You work or study together, hang out together, and share silly times. Later on, those same relationships will become your source of support. When you get married, those friends will stand with you. When you start a family, they'll congratulate you and lend a hand. When you face the tough times in life, they'll be there to lend a listening ear, a shoulder to cry on, and possibly the shirt off their backs.

Not all of them will be best friends. Some have already let you down; and others will later. That's because they're human, just like you. But they're still friends. They're still your greatest asset in life. Be a friend. Have friends. Keep friends.

Stock up on friends, and you'll never be poor.

Remember the four T's.

"Work while you have the light.
You are responsible
for the talent that has
been entrusted to you."

—Henri-Frederic Amiel

TIME, TALENT, TRUTH, TREASURE

Just as a table has four legs, your life has four important components. They are time, talent, truth, and treasure.

Time is your most limited asset. You have only twenty-four hours in each day and 365 days in each year. You have no idea how many of those years are in the bank. Spend your time wisely.

Talent is your gift from God, the thing or things you can do well. Value talent. Allow God to develop your talent, and use it for good. Your developed talent will earn your living and give you a worthwhile life.

Truth is the core of your character. If you are true to yourself and true to others, you will make a difference in your home, your school, and your workplace.

Treasure is your wealth. You will likely have more money than you'll need to survive; most Americans do. What you do with the extra will determine your legacy. Spend it wisely.

Time, talent, truth, and treasure—they're not food groups, but they will keep you healthy!

Learn to laugh at yourself.

"You can turn painful situations
around through laughter.
If you can find humor in
anything, even poverty,
you can survive it."

—Bill Cosby

HUMOR

"Laugh, and the world laughs with you," the poet said. That's especially true if you are laughing at yourself. Laughter is God's cure for gloomy days and tense situations. Watch, and you'll notice that a giggle will arise even in the most serious times.

One of the healthiest habits you can develop is a sense of humor. Laughter is good for your heart, physically, emotionally, and spiritually. Cultivate the ability to laugh in nearly every situation.

Above all, be willing to laugh at yourself. If you take yourself too seriously, you will feel uncomfortable around others. Share a good laugh when life puts an unexpected curb in front of your step, and others will be comfortable with their own trips.

It takes a good sense of self-worth to laugh at yourself. People who lack self-esteem are not able to do it. Those who are willing to poke fun at themselves once in awhile actually enhance their standing in the eyes of others.

As Mary Pettibone Poole once said, "He who laughs, lasts."

Simplify your life.

"Everything should be made
as simple as possible,
but not one bit simpler."

—Albert Einstein

SIMPLICITY

Take a look around your room. What do you see? Old clothes that you haven't worn in a year or two? School assignments that you turned in ages ago but never bothered to throw away? Old sports equipment that you never use anymore?

It's amazing the way things clutter our lives. And it's just beginning. Throughout your life you will acquire cars, furniture, clothing, equipment, and even homes. Much of it will be things you don't need. The things you own take up your time and energy as you attempt to store them, repair them, and search for more.

Begin the habit of traveling light. Before you make a purchase, ask yourself, *Do I really need this, or do I just want it?* At least once a year, look through your closets to determine what you can do without.

Buy fewer things. Buy what you need instead of what you want. Spend less money on the things you buy, and hold on to them for a shorter time.

The result will be that you live a simpler, more carefree life. As a bonus, you'll have more time and money with which to do good.

Wiser spending means cleaner closets and a cleaner heart!

Practice common courtesy.

"Good manners will
open doors that the best
education cannot."

—Clarence Thomas

MANNERS

Yes, sir. No, Ma'am. Please. Thank you. You're welcome.

Those words were once commonly heard in our society. Now they're as rare as a two-dollar bill. That's too bad, because they were more than just meaningless discipline. They were signs of the respect people had for one another.

Good manners are not a sign of being weak or old fashioned. They signify dignity and respect that all people deserve.

Cultivate the habit of being polite, even though doing so may place you in the minority. Look at others when they are speaking to you. Avoid interrupting. Always say thank you when you receive an invitation, even if you have no intention of accepting it. Address those older than you with titles of respect such as Sir, Ma'am, or Mister.

Does it seem that there are too many rules to remember? Let's boil it down to one. Treat others as you would like to be treated. That action alone will grant you respect from everyone.

Courtesy makes a circle, not a square.

Insure
your future.

"It is only when we truly
understand that we have a
limited time on earth that we
will live each day to the fullest."

—Elizabeth Kubler-Ross

PRECAUTION

This world of ours can be a wild and dangerous place at times. From traffic accidents to stock market crashes, the potential for harm surrounds us every day. Sometimes, survival seems to be a matter of pure luck.

It's not.

The older you grow—and the wiser—the more you will learn to look ahead, read the road, and prepare for the journey. Learn to take precautions.

Young and healthy as you are, it's hard to imagine that anything could happen to your vitality. While it seems unlikely now that you will ever need it, putting aside money for illness can only help.

If you love the outdoors, you probably enjoy pushing yourself to the limit. But everyone has a breaking point. Take precautions when you engage in sports. Use safety equipment.

Your brand new car is a pleasure to drive. And it should give you years of trouble-free performance. But cars eventually break down. Be wise. Set aside some money for car repairs.

I know what you're thinking. *Nothing bad is going to happen to me.* You can make that prediction even more certain by taking appropriate precautions for your future.

Never take God's blessings for granted.

"Gratitude is not only the greatest of virtues, but the parent of all others."

—Cicero

GRATITUDE

For the most part, we live in a world of plenty. We have plenty of food, plenty of clean drinking water, and plenty of opportunity.

The tragedy is that we so often behave as if we created these things. We didn't. They are gifts from God, and we dare not take them for granted.

All of us have abilities. We can do things that earn money and improve our lives. But which of us can say, "I created myself," or "I determined that I would be a good singer?"

We have plenty to eat, but which of us can say, "I made my own food grow?"

We depend on God for everything because He is the giver of life.

Develop the habit of giving thanks. Recognize that good gifts come from God, not self, and tell Him so!

"Lord, thank You for what You've given to me." Say that prayer each day, and you will find yourself content in every situation.

Only turkeys skip prayer on Thanksgiving Day.

Seek to become a person of excellence.

"The secret of joy in
work is contained in
one word—excellence.
To know how to do
something well is to enjoy it."

—Pearl S. Buck

EXCELLENCE

You can see it. You can feel it. Sometimes you can even taste it. Excellence— the quality that separates the meaningful from the mediocre.

You know what excellence looks like in an automobile, a suit of clothing, or a restaurant. What does it look like in a life?

Become a person of excellence. Do your best work every time, whether anybody is looking or not. Go the extra mile. Stay overtime to help with the clean-up. Work as if you were getting the kind of pay you really wanted.

Tell the truth, not because you have no alternative, but because you have a standard of honesty. Let your character be your walking resume.

Be on time so that people never have to wait for you.

Set a standard for yourself that is above average; then keep it.

Set yourself apart from others. The benefits may not come all at once, but there will be a payoff.

Besides, the air is cleaner at the front of the pack.

See the world.

"Certainly travel is more
than the seeing of sights;
it is a change that goes on,
deep and permanent,
in the ideas of living."

—Miriam Beard

TRAVEL

Do you love your hometown? I love mine. But I love to leave it too; I love to travel.

Travel broadens your horizons. It lets you see things you've never seen before. Travel opens your mind. It introduces you to new people, new cultures, and new traditions. Travel improves your self-confidence. It causes you to become comfortable in all kinds of situations. Travel adds to your knowledge base. You learn things while traveling that you can't learn from textbooks, lectures, or videos. Every country and every culture is a classroom where you can learn about life.

Now is the best time in your life to travel. When you are young, healthy, and free from long-term commitments, you can travel easily.

Travel overseas if you can. Accept business travel assignments whenever they're offered. Let your counselors, your supervisors, and your parents know that you are willing to take that assignment in the next city, state, or country.

See the world while you're young, and it will never grow old.

Build strong and lasting relationships.

"The only way to have
a friend is to be one."

—Ralph Waldo Emerson

NETWORK

If you want to have a friend, you've got to be one. Here's how to make strong friendships that will last as long as you do.

Be friendly. Be the first one to say hello. Engage others in conversation. Always have a cheerful word.

Be open. Talk even to the people you don't immediately like. Give people a chance to reveal their strengths. And when people are difficult, remain friendly—remembering that God loves them as much as He loves you.

Be interested. When you ask a question, listen to the answer. Allow people to talk. Take an interest in what they do, where they live, and who they are.

Be helpful. Everybody has a need. Some need companionship, others need assistance. Be aware of what people need, and help them get it. They'll return the favor when they can.

Be loyal. Never break a confidence. When others confide in you, let them know that you will respect their trust.

Work on your relationships. A good friendship network is better than a good car, a good home, or even a good education. Some will be high maintenance. Others will take less of your time and effort. But both are valuable to your character, personality, and potential.

Even a friend in need is a friend indeed.

Write out your life goals.

"In the absence of clearly
defined goals, we become
strangely loyal to performing
daily acts of trivia."

—Author Unknown

GOALS

What were you thinking about yesterday? It's hard to remember, isn't it? Things that dominated your mind only twenty-four hours ago are gone like a deleted computer file.

That same thing can happen to your life goals if you don't write them down.

Your goals are your road map for life. They are the high points you hope to hit, and they spell out your plan for getting there. That information is vital for your success. Write it down.

Sit down and ask God about His goals for your life. Then, write out these goals for the next year, for the next five years, for ten years, and for your entire life. That doesn't mean that you won't ever change directions, but it will help you stay on track. You will feel like you have a purpose and that life is more stable.

Writing out your goals will make them more real to you. It will also keep you accountable to work toward them. And don't forget to let God be your Global Positioning System (GPS). He already knows the route of your life—He's already been there.

A plan is your ticket to the future.

Stay humble.

"Life is a long lesson
in humility."

—James M. Barrie

HUMILITY

As a recent graduate, you have gained a lot of knowledge. Loads of information is still fresh in your mind. Your challenge will be to share that information without making yourself conceited or proud.

Most people would rather see what you have accomplished than *hear* about it. Let your actions speak for you. Show the marks of humility. Let the praise come for your efforts. Always be willing to learn.

Listen before you speak, especially around those who are older or have more experience than you. Allow their wisdom to be heard.

Be careful of saying "I told you so." Although it is sometimes true, no one likes to hear it.

Cultivate the habit of giving away the credit for things that you do as a team. Never be one to say, "That was my idea!" A humble person is always ready to give their blue ribbon to another.

Remember, if you put yourself in the hall of fame, there probably won't be many there for the ceremony.

Prepare a personal resume.

"People forget how fast you
did the job, but they remember
how well you did it."

—Howard Newton

JOB

I t's true, you never get a second chance to make a first impression. And these days, that first impression will probably be made by a piece of paper or an electronic document. Your resume introduces you to prospective employers.

Be brief. Highlight your experience on your resume, but don't give your entire life's history. Highlight the experiences that make you look fit for the job. Check out a book or two at the library on how to write a concise cover letter and an exciting resume.

Be thorough. As a recent graduate, you don't have much experience on the job. But you have done other things that show your ability to carry out tasks and lead others. List your extracurricular activities and involvement.

Be positive. Always present yourself with a smile. That goes for your resume also. Tell about the good things you've done. Leave out any criticisms of former employers.

Be truthful. It's tempting to inflate your achievements on paper. After all, who will know? Perhaps no one. But you will know, and God knows. Always tell the truth.

If it's well said, it will be well read.

Plan to read a good book once a month.

"What is reading but
silent conversation."

—Walter Savage Landor

RESEARCH

Now that you have graduated, you'll never have to study again, right? Wrong! Your education in the game of life is just beginning. You'll discover things about relationships, marriage, your career, raising children, and more!

Develop the habit of reading, not because you have to, but because you want to. Up until now, you've had assigned reading. Now you can choose your own reading material. As a rule, read a good book at least once a month.

Vary what you read. Read how-to books, Bible study books, leadership books, biography and history books, current novels, and classic literature. Make yourself a student of the world.

Here's a hint: get a library card. Most of the books that you'll want to read are there, and you can borrow them for free!

Mark Twain said that the person who doesn't read has no advantage over the person who can't read. You can, so do it. It'll open your mind and improve your life.

Readers are reapers.

Associate with the right people.

"Associate yourself with
men of good quality if you
esteem your own reputation,
for 'tis better to be alone
than in bad company."

—George Washington

QUALITY

It's true; birds of a feather really do flock together. You are free to associate with whomever you choose, but be aware that your relationships with others will define your life in many ways.

If you associate with leaders, you will become a leader.

If you associate with slackers, you will begin to look for shortcuts.

If you associate with people of high moral character, you will develop high standards.

If you associate with people who break the law, you will probably follow suit. Even if your intentions are good, the attitude and actions of others will ultimately affect your behavior.

Be aware that, for better or worse, others will judge you by the company you keep. That may be unfair, but it is certainly true.

Choose good friends. Go for quality instead of quantity. Have a cup of coffee with someone who knows something you want to learn. Take a trip to the mall with someone who can teach you about smart purchases and wise investments.

Quality people raise the achievement bar in life.

Walk daily with God.

"His delight is in the law of the Lord, and on his law he meditates day and night."

—Psalm 1:2

MEDITATION

Who is your best friend? And how did you get to know them? You probably started with a conversation; then you began to do things together. Before long, you were inseparable.

In the same way, you can develop a relationship with the most important person in your life, God. You'll never have a better friend. No one but God will ever go the last mile for you. Get to know Him.

Begin with conversation. Make it a habit to talk with God every day. Spend time telling Him what's on your mind; then listen for what He has to say to your inner spirit.

Start doing things together. When you take a walk, spend that time with God. Once in awhile, take an hour or two to go to your favorite quiet place, and spend the time alone with Him. Meditate by thinking about His love for you and your love for Him. Make plans together.

Before long, you'll become inseparable.

Emphasize the positive.

"The greatest discovery of my
generation is that a human
being can alter his life by
altering his attitude."

—William James

ATTITUDE

Is the glass half full or half empty? Since the glass doesn't know, the answer will be whatever you decide.

That's true of every situation you will face in life. The experience can be positive or negative depending on your reaction to it. How you see an event has almost as much impact as the event itself. For example, your reaction to the actions or attitudes of others can be for your benefit, even when their actions or attitudes are negative. God can use the negative or painful experiences you face in your life to teach you. He'll show you how faithful and dependable He is when you are without anyone else to turn to for help. He will be there. He'll also change your character and develop you into a calm and mature person.

So, make the decision to be a person who sees the positive side of everything. There are many reasons to do so. You'll feel better. Dwelling on problems will get you down. After awhile, you actually start to feel ill. Negative breeds negative. "Stinking thinking" can also affect your body as well as your emotions.

There's another reason to look on the bright side. Others will gravitate to you if you have a positive attitude. They'll avoid you if you are always negative.

Remember, there are more "half-fulls" than "half-emptys" in every situation. See for yourself!

Make thanksgiving a daily habit.

"No duty is more urgent than that of returning thanks."

—Ambrose of Milan

THANKSGIVING

Thanksgiving isn't just a holiday; it's a way of life. A proud person finds it difficult to be thankful because it means giving credit to someone else. A humble person loves to give thanks because that person recognizes that they depend on others.

That's certainly true of our relationship with God. He created the world and us. He gives us life, health, and all good things. Develop the life habit of saying thanks to Him.

That same principle applies to other areas in life. Give thanks to your friends when they are loyal or helpful. Give thanks to coworkers when they lend a hand and make your job easier. Give thanks to your boss for making a good decision.

That's "ThanksLIVING." And it's an observance that can be year-round. In fact, an attitude of thanksgiving will add years to your life. You'll be healthier. You'll have more friends. You'll have a better mental state.

Thank you very much.

Ask for forgiveness quickly.

"You are never so strong
as when you forgive."

—Kimberly Converse

FORGIVENESS

Are you perfect? If not, you'll do something wrong sooner or later. When that happens, you'll have two choices.

One, you can deny your responsibility, pretend that you've done nothing wrong, and refuse to make amends. Quite honestly, that's the natural tendency of human beings.

The other response is to admit your error, say you're sorry, and do what it takes to make things right. It doesn't come naturally, but it's the best way to respond when you've failed.

When you're wrong, say, "I'm sorry," and say it quickly. Let others know that you recognize your own fault. Doing so will disarm their anger and help them to move beyond the problem and into the process of reconciliation.

Then see what you can do to correct the situation. Sometimes there's nothing you can do beyond apologizing. But you can replace what you've broken or give back what you've stolen.

When you're in the wrong, admit it right away. Admitting your fault will save others the trouble of pointing it out to you.

Forgive now—forgiven later.

Discover a personal hobby.

"A hobby a day keeps
the doldrums away."

—Phyllis McGinley

HOBBY

If you're lucky, you'll wind up doing the thing that you love most for a living. There's no one more fortunate than an architect who loves to design or a singer who loves to sing. It's great when you can spend your days doing something enjoyable.

But you need hobbies too. Nobody can play for a living, and whatever you choose to do will soon become work. You need other interests to relieve stress and keep your mind fresh.

Look for other pursuits that will enrich your life. For some, sports fill that need. Golf, tennis, and basketball are great ways to stay in shape and relax.

For others, the arts are a perfect hobby. Painting, making music, or singing in church are all worthwhile things to do.

But whatever you choose, remember that it's not merely fun. Hobbies are a necessary part of life. Keep them in perspective, but keep them. You need them to stay healthy in life.

Work at having fun, and you'll have more fun at work.

Find a
stress buster.

"What is without periods
of rest will not endure."

—Ovid

RELAXATION

Count on these two things in life. First, you are going to experience stress. Second, you'll need to find a way to relieve it.

Everybody feels stress—the feeling of anxiety that results from an overloaded schedule, personal conflict, or other negative situations. Stress is a fact of life just like common colds, mosquito bites, or sunburns. It will happen! And you'll need to find a way to deal with it. The question is whether your coping mechanisms will be healthy or unhealthy.

Some people deal with stress by abusing alcohol or drugs, becoming angry, or withdrawing. Those are unhealthy methods of coping with stress. They take care of the stress symptoms, but not the root cause. And these methods add even more stress.

Others deal with stress by exercising, praying, or talking with friends. Those are healthy coping methods. However, handing your problems and stress over to God gives you the ability to relax and you can count on Him to work on the root cause of your stresses.

Dealing with stress takes a plan. First, identify the stress makers. Second, identify the stress relievers. And third, work on the stress relievers. Too simple? Remember what caused the stress in the first place, difficulty. So, try the alternative.

Stress is a mess that you can clean up.

Take care of yourself.

"Sleep is the golden chain
that ties health and
our bodies together."

—Thomas Dekker

HEALTH

How long do you want to live? Sixty years? Seventy? One hundred? No, you don't get to choose exactly how long you live, but there are some things you can do to extend and enjoy your life.

The health habits you develop now, while you are a young adult, are likely to be the ones you will keep for the rest of your life.

Eat right. "Junk food" is not just an expression; some foods really are worthless. They may taste good, but they have little nutritional value and can actually harm your health.

Get plenty of rest. You can stay up late, get up early, and work hard all day. You can, but that doesn't mean you should. Your body needs rest. You will do even better work with more sleep.

And don't forget exercise. That's the third leg on the triangle of health. Now that you're out of school, your life may settle into a more predictable routine, which may include becoming a couch potato. It'll be up to you to get off the couch and into the gym.

Proper diet, rest, and exercise; you can't live without them!

Always hold your head high.

"The man who has confidence in himself gains the confidence of others."

—Hasidic Saying

CONFIDENCE

Do you remember *The Little Engine That Could?* The little red train engine in the familiar children's story had to perform a difficult task—hauling a train to the top of the mountain. The chore was way beyond his ability, but he kept himself going with the steady chant, "I think I can; I think I can."

Sure enough, he did!

You can too. Never let anyone destroy your self-confidence. You're a capable, intelligent, successful person. You've just graduated from school, haven't you?

When you're tempted to become discouraged because of a failure or when you're facing a daunting task, remind yourself of what you've already achieved.

You have a lot going for you. For one, God believes in you. According to the Bible, He thinks you were wonderfully made. You've passed His inspection. He loves you.

Others also believe in you—parents, friends, teachers, pastors, and counselors. They have confidence in your ability to perform the tasks that you have been called and trained to do. Never stop believing in yourself.

You can do it, if you know you can.

Establish a personal budget.

"Make money your god, and it will plague you like the devil."

—Henry Fielding

FINANCES

It seems incredible. The government spends billions of dollars each year on defense, research, civil engineering, disaster relief, welfare, and a million other things. But how do they keep track of the money? How do they know how much to spend on each item?

They work from a budget. The spending for each year is carefully planned. The budget attempts to keep spending on track.

It can be the same for you. A personal budget will keep your personal finances on track, even though you won't be spending a billion dollars a year! A budget is simply a blueprint, a plan for spending and saving. Sticking to it means you will have the money available that you've planned on for entertainment, travel, and investment, as well as for your bills.

The budget keeps you in control of your finances, preventing impulse buying or silly spending decisions that can cause a financial disaster. A budget puts you in the driver's seat.

Control spending, or it will control you.

Exercise four times a week.

"All growth depends
on activity. There is no
development physically or
intellectually without effort,
and effort means work."

—Calvin Coolidge

PHYSICAL

Can it really be this easy? Can twenty minutes of exercise four times a week really keep your body in good physical condition?

Yes. If you watch what you eat and get plenty of rest, exercising four times a week will keep you in shape.

The problem is that working those four exercise periods into a busy week can be a challenge, especially if you have to drive to the gym to do it. It takes willpower, not so much to actually complete the exercise but to take the time away from other things. Remember that you are created in the image of God. You can do His work and yours better if you are healthy and in shape.

Build an exercise routine into your life right where you are. If you can't run at the gym, run around the block. If you can't join a fitness club, create one in your home. Weights can be made from cans of soup. You can jog in place if you don't have a treadmill. Crunches or push-ups will work just as well as that expensive strength machine.

Choose something that's easy and enjoyable.

A perfect fit doesn't just refer to your jogging outfit!

Take baby steps into tomorrow.

"If you paint in your mind
a picture of bright and
happy expectations, you put
yourself into a condition
conducive to your goal."

—Norman Vincent Peale

REALISTIC EXPECTATIONS

Rome wasn't built in a day, and you won't reach all of your life goals in a day either. In fact, you won't reach them in a week, a month, or a year. That's why they're called "life" goals: it takes a lifetime to realize them.

That means you'll need to set realistic expectations about what you can do today or tomorrow. Focus on baby steps, not giant leaps. If you think of each decision as an important step toward your future, they won't seem trivial or boring. Your goals will make everyday life worthwhile.

You can't complete a graduate degree today, but you can enroll in a program. You can't meet all of your financial goals today, but you can put another twenty dollars into your savings account.

You may not be able to get married today, but you can make some decisions about what type of person you hope to marry. You can't meet all of your career goals today, but you can develop your skills and research your interest fields.

Take your life one step at a time. You'll worry less and achieve more.

Do what you can today, and let God work on tomorrow.

Don't worry, be happy.

"Worry is a misuse
of imagination."

—Dan Zadra

WORRY

Would you ever choose to get the flu— or even a normal cold? If you could choose to stop experiencing back problems or being overweight, would you do it?

Nobody would willingly take on a health problem. We all want to be healthy.

But many of us choose to do something that is terribly unhealthy; something that affects our physical and emotional well-being in negative ways and offers nothing in return. We choose to worry.

Worry has an impact on your health. It contributes to headaches, stomach problems, back problems, acne, fatigue, and depression.

And worry doesn't pay. Can worrying add a day to your life? Can it put more money into your bank account? Obviously, it is a purely negative behavior, yet we often choose it.

Here's the thing. If you can choose to worry, you can choose *not* to. Make up your mind that you will not spend your time worrying over things that you cannot control. Have a positive outlook. That's something you can control!

Happiness isn't just a condition; it's a choice.

Discover
your gift.

"The glorious gifts of God

are not to be cast aside."

—Homer

GIFTEDNESS

What is your spiritual gift? It is the ability or abilities that God has especially given to you in order to benefit others.

God gives everyone who believes in Him a special ability. Some are gifted leaders; others are good at speaking or teaching. Some are good at helping or encouraging others. Some are blessed with the ability to manage money; some are given the ability to exercise extraordinary faith. The God who created you gifted you. There is something *you* can do to make the world a better place. You have talents that can be used to create a better community, or at least a better neighborhood.

Your special abilities can help your church grow. They can help a child understand spiritual things. They can bring healing to the sick and help to the helpless.

You have a gift. Ask God or a close friend what your spiritual gift is. You need to find out and begin to use it to serve those around you.

Your spiritual gift doesn't have a long shelf life.

Face your insecurities head on.

"There is no security on
this earth, there is
only opportunity."

—General Douglas MacArthur

SECURITY

Do you face your insecurities head on? Some people hide from them. They know what causes them to be afraid or uncomfortable, and they avoid these situations at all costs.

Others choose to ignore or deny their insecurities. They place their heads in the sand and pretend that nothing is wrong.

There's a better way to deal with unpleasant circumstances—meet them head on. If you're afraid of public speaking or teaching, volunteer to read Scripture in church. If you feel insecure about your finances, take a course on budgeting. If you're uncomfortable thinking about death, volunteer to visit a nursing home.

Don't hide from the hard things in life, and don't ignore them. Meet them head on, and work through them. And remember, you don't face them alone. God is aware of the things that concern you. He knows your fears. But do you know His strength? Do you understand how very much He wants to equip you to meet the challenges in your life?

Your insecurities are afraid of your faith!

Be responsible in the small things of life.

"Leadership is doing what is right when no one is watching."

—George Van Valkenburg

INTEGRITY

A farmer took a truckload of grain to market, drove his truck onto the scales, and hopped out to stand beside it. Just as the scale operator looked down for a moment, the farmer stepped onto the scale beside his truck, adding his weight to the weight of his crop. A moment later, the scale operator stepped out around the corner and handed the farmer his scale ticket. As he did, he said with a smile, "I thought you might like to know, you just sold yourself for $2.60."

People "sell themselves" by making little choices that lack integrity. Make it your aim to be honorable in all things, even the little things in life. Be a person of integrity. People may or may not see what you do, but your Father in Heaven watches in love.

Always tell the truth.

Never turn in false numbers on your expense account.

If you are not ill, don't steal a day from your employer by saying that you are. Integrity is formed by small choices, not large ones.

Be honest in the little things, and you'll be honest in the big ones too.

Read the Bible daily.

"To acquire knowledge, one must study, but to acquire wisdom, one must observe."

—Marilyn Von Savant

DEVOTIONAL LIFE

It takes only five minutes a day. That's all the time you need to read a chapter or two of the Bible, and that's a daily habit that will go a long way toward ensuring your spiritual health.

The Bible is God's Word, the only reliable source of truth in a world of confusing voices. Read it to understand.

The Bible is a source of strength, God's comfort in a world of troubling circumstances. Read it for encouragement.

The Bible is a mirror, able to penetrate the deepest corners of your soul. Read it for wisdom.

The Bible is an engaging story, telling the history of God's creation and His interaction with it. Read it for enlightenment.

The Bible is a love letter, telling the story of God's affirmation and acceptance of you, just as you are. Read it for courage.

The Bible is a will and testament, giving you the assurance of an inheritance after you die. Read it for hope.

Five minutes a day—the best time of your life.

Place your mind over matter.

"The mind is the battleground
on which every moral and
spiritual battle is fought."

—J. Oswald Sanders

MASS MEDIA

Do you use the media, or does the media use you?

Television, the Internet, movies, radio, music, and other media enrich our lives immensely. Can you imagine living without music? How much more corrupt would our society be without the watchful eye of the news media?

Yet since the mass media dominates our attention so effectively, it's easy for the tail to begin wagging the dog—for the media to control rather than merely enrich our lives.

It's been estimated that the average person watches television for more than twenty hours per week. That's far too much time for most healthy, productive adults. Limit the time you spend in front of the tube. Use it for entertainment and information, not vegetation.

The Internet allows the free flow of useful information all around the world. But it also allows the free flow of harmful images into our homes—into our minds. Make a deal with yourself; agree that you will not allow yourself to view things over the Internet that you would not feel comfortable with in other settings.

The news media provides helpful, accurate information about everything from weather forecasts to world conflicts. Yet it can also provide distorted views and biased opinions. Let others gather the facts, but learn to interpret those facts for yourself.

It's better to spend time living life than watching or hearing about it.

Plan to be a lifelong learner.

"The strongest principles
of growth lie in the
human choice."

—George Eliot

PERSONAL GROWTH

The best thing you can learn at school is how much you don't know. Far from being finished, your education is only beginning. They don't call it "commencement" for nothing!

The most successful people continue their education far beyond graduation day. They are lifelong learners. They continue to improve their minds by gaining new knowledge, trying new experiences, and meeting new people. You can become a lifelong learner too.

Develop a curiosity about your culture. Look and listen to people you meet. Be aware of your surroundings without becoming consumed by them.

Read constantly. Have at least one good book going at all times. Read book reviews. Stop by the library. Join a reading group. Open your mind to some refreshing new thoughts.

Sign up for a class just for the fun of it. You'll learn a new skill or hobby and probably make a few friends. For example, enroll in a class on computer science, photography, or cooking. A wise woman once told me she took each decade as a chance to learn a new hobby.

Travel. Visit new places, museums, and concerts. The world is a wonderful, exciting place. Explore it! Discover it! Enjoy it!

You won't be a couch potato if you're on the *grow.*

Open your heart to worship.

"Let everything that has breath praise the LORD."

—Psalm 150:6

PRAISE

You do it naturally nearly every day. You praise your coworkers for a job well done. You compliment a date on their appearance. You congratulate friends on their achievements. So why not extend that habit of giving praise to God in worship?

Just as your mind and your body need exercise to be healthy, so does your soul—your inner person. Worship God by acknowledging who He is and what He has done. He is the Creator of the universe. Yet He is a personal and loving Heavenly Father concerned with the details of your life.

Develop the habit of beginning and ending your day in worship, praising God for what He has done. When you praise God, it is harder to worry about the problems in life.

Take it to the next level. Let your entire life be an offering of praise to God. Imitate God by living a life of moral purity, integrity, and honesty. Be kind to others, work hard, and conduct yourself with dignity under stress.

A grateful heart is a terrible thing to waste!

Save yourself
for marriage.

"Purity in person and in
morals is true Godliness."

—Hosea Ballou

PURITY

When does a healthy marriage begin? Does it start at the altar, when you pledge yourself to your spouse? Or does it begin when you are dating, when you and your future partner are getting to know one another and forming the bond that will eventually become a faithful marriage?

Or does it begin even earlier?

In fact, it begins now, even though you may not have met your future spouse yet. Respect, integrity, purity—these are characteristics that you must have in order to be happily married. You can cultivate them now.

Respect the people you date as if they were your marriage partners. One of them may be someday.

Keep yourself morally pure. Don't deceive a dating partner by pretending to be more interested in marriage than you are, and don't pressure him or her sexually.

If you want to be happily married fifty years from now, start now, even if you're not seeing anyone at the moment.

Save the best for later, and later you'll have the best.

Seek wise counsel from the experts.

"Common-sense in an uncommon degree is what the world calls wisdom."

—Samuel Taylor Coleridge

WISDOM

Some people think that the wisest person is the one who knows all the answers. I disagree. The wisest person is the one who deals with all the questions.

Realistically, there's no way you can have all the knowledge or insight that you need to navigate life. In order to survive on planet earth, you need expertise in subjects like healthcare, finances, insurance, education, parenting, spirituality, and auto mechanics, just to name a few.

Is there any way one human being can master all of those subjects?

Don't try to memorize all the answers. Instead, develop a network of advisors and mentors who can give you the advice you need. For many people, that network begins with Mom and Dad. They've been alive longer than you and that experience is valuable. Tap into it.

Keep in touch with teachers whom you respect, and seek mentors. You can't do everything life requires of you alone, and you don't have to. And don't forget, the best source of wisdom is the Bible.

When you need directions in life, stop and ask.

Be happy
with yourself.

"Insist on yourself,
never imitate. Every
great man is unique."

—Ralph Waldo Emerson

UNIQUENESS

There is only one of you, and that's exactly the way God wants it. He made you unique. You truly are one of a kind. That's something to celebrate.

All of us have a limitation or two. Likewise, we all have something we can do as well, or better, than anyone else. Take notice of the things you do well. They're gifts that God has given you.

Celebrate your birthday. It's a good thing that you're alive! The world is a better place because you were born. You bring something unique to the planet.

Enjoy your own sense of humor, tastes, and interests. They're the things that make you different from the rest of the crowd.

Above all, don't wish to be someone else. Avoid the trap of believing that other people are more beautiful, more talented, smarter, and more delightful than you. You are a unique person, a special person. Be glad that you are you.

There's nobody in the place with your kind of grace!

Never lose hope.

"Faith is putting all your
eggs in God's basket, then
counting your blessings
before they hatch."

—Romona C. Carroll

FAITH

You can't live without it. It's the one thing that is vital to sustain your life; therefore, it is invaluable.

You can live without money. It's difficult, but there are many poor people who survive in the world. You won't die if you run out of cash.

You can live without fame; nearly everyone does.

You can even live without love. Loneliness is painful, but it is not fatal.

But you cannot live without hope. It is the life's blood of the soul. If you need food to keep your body alive, you also need hope to keep your spirit living.

Never lose hope, though you may be tempted to. You may fail, but your failure is not fatal. Do not lose hope.

You may be abandoned, but you are not alone. Do not lose hope. You may suffer, but your suffering has purpose. Hold on to your faith. It will sustain you. It will strengthen you. It will preserve your soul.

Keep hope alive. You can't live without it.

Know your ABCs.

"If we confess our sins, he is
faithful and just and will
forgive us our sins and purify
us from all unrighteousness."

—1 John 1:9

THE PLAN OF SALVATION

Years ago, you learned your ABCs. Not long after that, you learned your 1,2,3s. Those are the basic building blocks of your education. You'll use them as long as you live.

There is another set of basic information that you need in life—the ABCs of salvation; the basics of how we relate to God. They're in the Bible. Look them up for clearer understanding.

A—Admit that you are a sinner. (Romans 3:23).

B—Believe that God sent Jesus to pay the punishment for your sin. (John 1:12).

C—Confess that you are sorry for sin and declare that Jesus Christ is now Number One in your life. (Romans 10:9-10).

A suggested prayer:

Lord Jesus, I admit that I have sinned against You. I am sorry for my sin, and I trust You to forgive me. I invite You to come into my life and help me to live for You all the days of my life. Amen.

It's that simple. You can be forgiven, loved, and free.

Learn your ABCs by accepting Jesus today.

Learn to be responsible.

"The price of greatness is responsibility."

—Sir Winston Churchill

RESPONSIBILITY

"**It's** not my job!" You've probably heard someone say that. If so you were listening to someone who will struggle all of their life. Winners accept responsibility. On the job, in the classroom, in a dorm room, at home—whatever they're expected to do, they simply do it.

Responsibility is a character quality that needs to be developed if you plan to succeed in your education, career, or relationships. It isn't a natural characteristic. Nearly everyone has a natural tendency to skip the hard parts in life. It's easier to let someone else do it than it is to roll up our sleeves and do it ourselves.

Every successful venture begins with someone who says, "That's my job." This person accepts responsibility for their own actions, and for the actions of those he or she may supervise.

Do you have interest in medicine, industry, politics, or sports? Start small. Do your homework. Do your job. Pay your bills. The habits you develop now will turn into the honors you receive later on.

Responsibility is spelled with a "U"!

Say those three little words.

"The best proof of love is trust."

—Dr. Joyce Brothers

LOVE

You may think we live in a "four letter word" society. We don't. It's a "three words" world. "I love you" are still the most important words that can come out of your mouth. And they are the most important words someone else will hear.

Love needs an expression. We can't just do nice things for those who matter most in our lives. We need to express our inner feelings for them.

You know what a difference it makes when you hear those words. The sun shines on an otherwise cloudy day. A window opens on an otherwise hopeless situation. The warm fuzzies take over an otherwise cold atmosphere.

If the words, "I love you," mean that much to you, imagine what a difference they'll make to another—your family members, your best friends, your spouse. Telling someone how much they mean to you is a sign of maturity.

Say those words carefully. Saying them is like ringing a bell; the sound can never be retrieved.

When the time is right, just say it!

Get right to
the point.

"Strong lives are motivated
by dynamic purpose."

—Kenneth Hildebrand

PURPOSE

"**W**hat's your point?" That's a good question. Why are you doing what you do, or saying what you say? Everything in life has a definite time, a definite place, and a definite purpose.

A person who "gets right to the point" is a person who understands the steps to success in life. Defining why you are doing something is always a good place to start. It keeps your thoughts and actions from wandering. It gives you a direction, and a direction helps you reach your goal.

How do you determine what your purpose should be? Is it right? Does it bring health, or does it bring harm to a situation or to another person. Is it helpful? Will it make the world around you a better place? Is it pure? Is it selfish? Does it seek to honor God? Is it harmful to another? Is it powerful? Will it motivate you to accomplish something else?

Drive without purpose is a wreck waiting to happen!

Send God an instant message.

"Prayer doesn't change things.
It changes people, and
they change things."

—Author Unknown

PRAYER

Online instant messaging puts you in touch with your best friends. You can say what's on your mind with just a few keystrokes. You also can learn what's on someone else's mind. But IMs are simply a new take on an old method of communicating friend-to-friend—prayer.

You don't need a keypad to talk to the best Friend you will ever have. God doesn't need the Internet to listen to you, or to talk to you. He uses prayer. Prayer is as natural as breathing and just as simple. Anytime and anywhere, you can tell your best Friend what's on your mind.

Talk to Him daily. Keep the communication line open. Don't wait until your mind and your heart gets cluttered with stuff. Talk to Him now.

Talk to Him plainly. Be honest about your feelings. Talk to Him about the things that make you angry, sad, or glad. He understands better than any earthly friend.

When you're praying, you're on *life* support!

Be a good citizen.

"And so, my fellow Americans,
ask not what your country can
do for you; ask what you
can do for your country."

—John F. Kennedy

CITIZENSHIP

You don't have to like everything that goes on in your country to be a good citizen. Let's face it, very human people run this nation. And humans make errors in judgment. Citizenship goes beyond being in one political party or another. And you can be a good citizen without wearing a political pin.

How?

Respect the land. You don't have to be an environmental extremist to simply take care of the land that God has given you. You already know what can be done to make your community a better and more attractive place to live. Just do it!

Vote. Go to the polls on Election Day. You have one of the most important privileges in the world, the right to voice your opinion on a ballot.

Be a leader. Offer your talents at some grassroots level in leading a project that will make life easier for someone less fortunate than you.

Citizenship is red, white, blue, and YOU.

Be as loyal as a puppy.

"You've got to give loyalty
down, if you want loyalty up."

—Donald T. Regan

LOYALTY

Your puppy will stand by you no matter what. Puppies are like that. Sometimes they aren't fed on time. Sometimes people trip over them. Sometimes they receive less than royal treatment. But puppies will be loyal anyway, no matter what the circumstances are.

That's a good way for humans to live as well!

Loyalty is a sign that someone is making personal progress. Is it you? Are you learning to stand by your family, your friends, your coworkers, or your organization?

Congratulations! You're taking a step in the direction of personal success. Winners don't drift with the tide or fly with the wind. They'll stand against almost anything to stand *by* something (or someone).

Be loyal in your heart. Once you give your allegiance, stick with it.

Be loyal in your conversation. Defend your friends with your words.

Be loyal in your actions. Make an effort to show someone you are on his or her side. Do something nice, without expecting recognition or reimbursement.

Loyalty is more than cool; it's courageous.

Keep the family tree trimmed.

"Many men can make a
fortune, but very few
can make a family."

—J. S. Bryan

FAMILY

You can tell a lot about people by the way they trim their trees. A property owner who doesn't make an effort to keep their property well landscaped speaks to their neighborhood without saying a word.

How about your family tree?

At every stage of your life, you will interact with some family member. From infancy to assisted living, you will probably have some contact with a relative.

Here are some tips for the care and keeping of the family tree.

Be friendly. It would be great if all relationships were super; but some aren't. Keep the lines of communication open, as best you can. Don't let situations keep you from speaking.

Be loyal. Stand alongside your family, no matter what. They've probably seen you through a few problem times. Look for a good time to return the favor.

Be available. There are things that only you can do for your family. You know them best, so you can help them most.

Family time may involve overtime, but it's prime time.

Go for the gold.

"Competition is a painful thing,
but it produces great results."

—Jerry Flint

COMPETITION

You don't have to win to be a winner. The person with the silver medal may have put more effort into the competition than the one wearing the gold. The difference is in trying.

Competition isn't something you have to fear. It can actually fuel your dreams and bring them to a reality. Competition is only dangerous when it is the driving factor in your life—when you are consumed with it and by it.

A competitive spirit is behind almost every great venture. For example, automobile dealers actually *prefer* to have other dealerships near them. Comparison shopping brings customers to their car lot.

As another example, you are aware of some brand name food, clothing, or electronic item because someone dared to dream of a bigger, better, or tastier product.

You don't have to be *the* best in order to be in the competition. You just have to be *your* best. Use your God-given intelligence, your skills, your training, and your network of associates, and go for the gold.

Remember, third place doesn't mean you're third-rate!

Keep climbing.

"We advance on our
journey only when we
face our goal, when we
are confident and believe
we are going to win out."

—Orison Swett Marden

ADVANCEMENT

Graduation isn't the last step. It's the first. Where you go from here depends on what you're willing to do. If you determine in your heart that you're on the path to personal success, you're on the right road.

Making the best of it, and making the best *out* of it represent the low road and the high road of life. Take the high road. Keep climbing. No matter what obstacles you may face, keep going! Don't be afraid to do more work. Make the best out of life.

Keep climbing academically. Now you know how to study. You know what it takes to make good grades. You know what it takes to make progress by gaining knowledge. Take it to the next level. If you're a high school graduate, advance to college graduation. If you're a college grad, advance to a graduate degree.

Keep climbing professionally. Whether it's your first day on the job or it's your first opportunity for a promotion, keep climbing. Keep your skills fresh. Stay alert to trends. Watch others; copy the best of the best.

Your stepping stone was someone else's obstacle.

Give and
receive respect.

"Carve your name on hearts
and not on marble."

—Charles Spurgeon

RECOGNITION

Some think it is better to give honor than to receive it. Do both. Learning to pay your respects is as important as receiving them yourself. You are motivated by praise, and so are your friends and associates. The lessons you learn about complimenting the efforts of others, and acknowledging your own efforts, will be of great value.

Give recognition. "Good job!" may be one of the most important sentences you will ever say out loud. People want to know that they matter in the home, in the classroom, on the job, or on the athletic field. You can be the one who will make a difference in someone's life. Just by recognizing the efforts of others, you can help their self-esteem, as well as motivate them to even greater efforts.

Receive recognition. People enjoy giving a unique and specific compliment. By blowing off the sincere compliments of others, you are depriving them of a chance to express themselves and, in another way, telling them that their evaluation is second rate. Also, by ignoring honor paid to you, you are failing to acknowledge your own self-worth and the honest efforts you have made.

Accept the gold medal. Later on, when someone ignores your work, you'll need to pull it out as a reminder to yourself.

Keep your life neat.

"Chaos and order are not enemies, only opposites."

—Richard Garriott

ORDER

You've probably been told to straighten your room once or twice. Did you know that a straightened life is just as important? Clutter doesn't just keep you from finding your socks or your favorite shirt; it also hinders your success in life. If you cannot keep clutter from ruling your life, it is time to reorganize, focus on what matters most, and give up some responsibilities.

Keep your personal life in order. Eat right. Sleep enough. Get some exercise. Get to school or work on time. Make notes as reminders. Keep track of birthdays and anniversaries.

Keep your professional life in order. Plan your work. Keep accurate files and records. Turn in your projects on time or in advance. Dress appropriately. Do what you're told to do, without complaining. Remember names. Be the first to praise someone on his or her advancement.

Order is a reflection of your character. By outwardly putting things in their place, you'll form habits that will keep your inner self neat. For example, a clean room, a straightened office space, or a well-kept automobile is a step toward an uncluttered heart and mind. Your personal habits affect all of your life, not just cubicles of it.

Keep things in their place, and there'll be a place for you.

Remember your history.

"So live that your memories
will be part of your happiness."

—Author Unknown

MEMORIES

Don't you just hate it when your mom drags out those pictures of you—the ones when you were in the first grade? It may make you uncomfortable, but it brings comfort to her. Why? Each step of your life has had its good moments, good memories.

I don't know what you have to do to keep your memories alive, but just do it. Think back over your life, even as you're looking ahead.

Remember the good times. You'll have enough challenging times to balance the good and bad. But remember the good ones.

Remember when you were free to laugh about yourself without feeling like everyone was looking at you; when you weren't afraid to try new things; when you realized you were growing up.

Don't keep a lid on your memories, even the bad ones. Grow by them. See how far you've come. A scrapbook, a photo album, videos—don't be afraid of them. Use them as reference points for your future.

History is just as important as current events.

Plan today for tomorrow.

"When your outgo exceeds your income, your upkeep becomes your downfall."

—William Aaron Toler

SAVINGS

Here's a good rule to live by. From your income, give God His due: give your church ten percent, a tithe. From what remains, give yourself your due: place ten percent of your income in long-term savings. Start that habit now, and it will serve you well for a lifetime.

Saving money makes sense for many reasons. For one, it's simply wise to spend less than you make. Too many people are doing the opposite, spending more than their income by borrowing heavily. Consumer debt is at an all-time high—and so is the number of reported bankruptcies. Don't overspend your income, and you won't have credit trouble.

Another reason to save is you never know what the future holds. The proverbial "rainy day" usually comes sooner or later in the form of a car repair bill, a layoff notice, or a health problem.

A third reason to save is you do know what the future holds, retirement. Not for many years, of course, but you will retire someday. How foolish it would be to arrive at that day completely unprepared. And for those times when you cannot be prepared, God will provide. He delights in watching out for His children.

Invest in savings now, and you'll have a secure future.

Watch what you wear.

"Beware so long as
you live, of judging
people by appearances."

—La Fontaine

APPEARANCE

These words were embossed on the mirror by the employee lounge of a store: "Your appearance reflects your attitude." It's true. How you feel about yourself inwardly shows up in how you dress. And you really can dress for success. How?

Dress confidently. A future employer may look at your sloppy clothes and decide that you will do your work just as sloppily. Be confident about your clothing. Let it say, "I'm qualified for this assignment!" and you'll feel that way.

Dress appropriately. The dress code may be spelled out in the employee manual, or it may not. Don't take any chances. Dress in a way that reflects your profession, in a way that says, "I'm available for that promotion!"

Dress conservatively. Clothing is expensive. Look for bargains. Consider buying from a consignment shop that has nearly new clothes. You don't need to spend hundreds to look like a million!

Your appearance does make a difference—especially to yourself. Make a fashion statement, and let that statement be, "I feel good about myself."

No shirt, no shoes, no future!

Always do your best.

"Regardless of what you are doing, if you pump long enough, hard enough, and enthusiastically enough, sooner or later the effort will bring forth the reward."

—Zig Ziglar

EFFORT

No one ever received a failing grade for making an effort. Many bad grades have been handed out for a lack of effort, however. Effort isn't just important at high school or university. It's important everywhere.

By making an effort, by always doing your best, you give yourself an advantage. At times, life is unfair. People get jobs, promotions, or relationships they seemingly don't deserve and sometimes without much effort. But as a rule, those who make an effort are those who make a difference.

Do the best you can.

Prepare yourself. Get all the education you can. Get all the training you can. And accept all the advice you can. The effort you put into your preparation will show up later in your performance.

Stretch yourself. You can do it! You can go to that next grade level, be a supervisor, get that scholarship, land that job. It can be yours by trying harder, working smarter, and stretching yourself mentally, spiritually, and physically.

You can't do more than your best!

Adjust to the
bad times.

"Prosperity is a great teacher,

adversity a greater."

—William Hazlitt

ADVERSITY

It would be great if all of our days were partly sunny. Obviously they're not. Sometimes there are storms—scary storms. How you react to them will determine whether you'll make it through them. Here are a few tips.

Expect bad times. Adversity is as certain as flies at a picnic! It's a fact of life that goes all the way back to the Garden of Eden. So don't be surprised when life turns partly cloudy—when you don't get that scholarship; when there's a downsizing at your corporation; when you get a negative report from the doctor's office.

Adjust to bad times. You'll have to go to Plan B. But go ahead; make the adjustments. Just because you have a limp doesn't mean you're out of the game. Make it part of your strategy for winning.

Trust God in the bad times. God is bigger than your problem. Trust His peace, wisdom, strength, healing, and companionship. You'll never know what God can do for you until you depend on Him—totally.

Bad times make big hearts.

Hit the books.

"I will study and get ready, and
perhaps my chance will come."

—Abraham Lincoln

STUDY

Wisdom is like a cold; you get it from someone. History has given us something positive: the knowledge of thousands printed in books and magazines. If you want to expand your mind, mind your reading. Hit the books.

Your study habits will, to a great degree, determine your path to success. For some, studying is a breeze. For others, it's a hurricane. You may be somewhere in between. But know this: you have to work at it. You have to discipline yourself to learn.

Study doesn't just come in spans of four years or twelve. It is a lifelong commitment. Every area of your life will demand wisdom that you don't already have.

You'll study to earn a degree.

You'll study to get a job (or keep it).

You'll study to improve your relationships.

You'll study to know God more.

So study well. Set a time. Choose a place. Zero in. Assemble resources. Keep notes. Discipline your efforts.

Hit the books before you hit the bricks!

Determine your beliefs.

"Strong values build
strong men, and then
make them stronger."

—Author Unknown

VALUES

If you don't absolutely believe in something, you'll fall for anything. There are some values that are not only worth living for, they're worth dying for. Determine what they are.

What do you believe about moral character? Are there things you refuse to do simply because they are wrong? Much of society says that everything is relative. But a world without boundaries is confusing and dangerous.

What do you believe about truth? May I say that I believe God's Word, the Bible, is absolutely true? It is my source for the forgiveness of my past and my source of hope for the future. Why? God, who inspired the Bible's writers to put it to the page, is absolutely holy and true. Those are my truth values. How about yours?

What do you believe about destiny? Do you have a purpose—a purpose that guides your actions, attitudes, and affiliations? Are there things you refuse to do because they will hinder your life goals?

Those are values, and values are valuable!

Keep a positive perspective.

"People never change,
only their perspectives."

—Sarah Crowder

OUTLOOK

We live in a battery-powered world. From your PDA to your MP3 player, the Energizer Bunny is working overtime. Batteries work great unless they're inserted in your electronic device the wrong way. They must be installed according to the positive and negative signs that are usually stamped on the device.

It's the same in life. It doesn't work if you put the negative where there should be a positive. A positive perspective always makes things work better.

Positive people are energizers. You might also notice that they are usually in leadership positions.That's a good thing to copy. Be a victor, not a victim. How? Look for the best in each situation. There's something to learn, and there's someone to share it with, God. Look for the best in others. Look past their faults to their finer characteristics. Look for the best in yourself. God made you; and He does good work.

Be positively positive, and you'll have a positive effect on others.

A positive outlook will make life more enjoyable.

Do good deeds.

"The end result of kindness is
that it draws people to you."

—Anita Roddick

KINDNESS

Who are some of the most important people in your life? Would you agree that part of the reason they are important is that they treat you right? Absolutely. Good deeds make good memories.

Good deeds are an act of gratitude. You are at this point in your life because someone made an investment in you: love, affirmation, finances, encouragement, friendship. You can capitalize on that investment by doing the same to others.

Good deeds are an act of maturity. Childish people are need oriented, and the need is usually theirs. Maturity focuses on others. It looks for ways to brighten someone else's life, to lighten someone else's burden.

Good deeds are an act of love. Random acts of kindness are fun ways to express your affection. Buy a stranger lunch, or hand out sodas at the park. "Show me the money!" the saying goes. Good deeds do just that; they are positive and tangible proofs of your commitment.

You have a window of time to show someone you care about them and about the investments they have made in your life.

Good deed? Good work!

Never give up.

"Press on! Nothing can take
the place of perseverance."

—Calvin Coolidge

PERSEVERANCE

Winners aren't necessarily braver than others; they're just braver for a longer period of time. They keep going. They never give up. If that can be said of you, then you have the ingredients to be a winner in whatever field you enter.

There are many reasons to quit. Physical, financial, or emotional setbacks can wear you out. But none of them is more important than persevering.

Perseverance is important because of what it does for you. When you refuse to give in to your circumstances, you prove your self-worth. When you muster the strength to persist in spite of your problems, you end up with a better opinion of yourself.

Perseverance is important because of what it does for others. Your refusal to give up may be just the example someone with a problem equal to, or greater than, yours really needs. "If they can do it, so can I!"

Throughout your career, you'll be tempted to quit. But never give up.

Don't let your problems be your king. Make them your subjects.

Keep a journal.

"May the words of my mouth
and the meditation of
my heart be pleasing in
your sight, O LORD, my
Rock and my Redeemer."

—Psalm 19:14

REFLECTION

You can see where you are going by looking at where you've been. Journaling is a good way to do that. Keeping a daily journal of your thoughts and activities is a good way to manage your time and monitor progress toward your personal goals. If you miss a day or two, don't worry; just go back to writing without feeling guilty. It takes a while to work into a habit.

Keep it simple. Whether you use a three-ring binder or a leather journal, don't set the bar too high. Keep your writing to a minimum, and it will be easier to make journaling a daily habit.

Keep it standard. Use the same format. Along with the date, include your reflections on the events of the day. Make observations. Set goals. Note highlights.

Keep it straight. Be honest with yourself. Your journal can be a mirror into your soul. Express yourself. Discipline yourself. Keep yourself in line.

Keep it silent. Your journal is for your eyes only. Your observations are personal and should be kept that way.

Journaling will not only help you keep track; it will keep you *on* track!

Be an example.

"Be as careful of the books you
read as the company you keep;
for your habits and character
will be as much influenced by
the former as by the latter."

—Paxton Hood

CHARACTER

The words to a Sunday School song come to mind: "What you are speaks so loud that the world can't hear what you say." That song wasn't about speeches; it was about character. Your life example is worth more than the credits on your resumé.

People will remember you had character long after they have forgotten how cute you were. Your value system will be far more important than your stock portfolio when someone looks back on your life.

Character is what you are when no one is watching. It's your life quality. It can't be bought or borrowed. You have to build it.

You build character by your choices—your daily decisions. The easy way or the right way? The choice is yours, and it's an important decision.

You build character by your disciplines. It doesn't matter if "Everybody's doing it!" Your refusal to let others determine your life direction is a discipline that will lead to exemplary character.

Setting a good example is worth more than setting a world record.

About the Author

Stan Toler is senior pastor of Trinity Church of the Nazarene in Oklahoma City, Oklahoma, and hosts the television program, "Leadership Today." For several years he taught seminars for Dr. John Maxwell's INJOY Group, a leadership development institute. Toler has written over 50 books, including his best-sellers, *God Has Never Failed Me, But He's Sure Scared*  *Me to Death a Few Times; The Buzzards Are Circling, But God's Not Finished With Me Yet; The Five-Star Church;* his popular *Minute Motivators* series; and his latest book, *The Secret Blend.*

To Contact the Author

Stan Toler
P.O. Box 892170
Oklahoma City, OK 73189-2170
E-mail: stoler1107@aol.com
Website: www.StanToler.com

Additional copies of this and other Honor Books products are available wherever good books are sold.

Minute Motivators for Leaders
Minute Motivators for Dieters
Minute Motivators for Teens
Minute Motivators for Teachers
Minute Motivators for Graduates

If you have enjoyed this book, or if it has had an impact on your life, we would like to hear from you.

Please contact us at:

HONOR BOOKS
Cook Communications Ministries, Dept. 201
4050 Lee Vance View
Colorado Springs, CO 80918
Or visit our Web site:
www.cookministries.com

HONOR ⓗⓑ BOOKS
Inspiration and Motivation for the Season of Life